12334

DATE DUE

Discard

★THE AMERICAN PROMISE★

Also by Milton Meltzer

American Politics: How It Really Works
Poverty in America
Crime in America
Ain't Gonna Study War No More: The Story of America's Peace-Seekers
Never to Forget: The Jews of the Holocaust
Rescue: The Story of How Gentiles Saved Jews in the Holocaust
Starting from Home: A Writer's Beginnings
The American Revolutionaries: A History in Their Own Words
Voices from the Civil War
The Black Americans: A History in Their Own Words
The Jewish Americans: A History in Their Own Words
George Washington and the Birth of Our Nation
Benjamin Franklin: The New American
Columbus and the World Around Him
The Bill of Rights: How We Got It and What It Means

★　　　★　　　★

BANTAM BOOKS
NEW YORK · TORONTO · LONDON · SYDNEY · AUCKLAND

THE
AMERICAN
PROMISE

Voices of a
Changing Nation
1945–Present

Edited by Milton Meltzer

★ ★ ★ ★

THE AMERICAN PROMISE
A Bantam Book / October 1990

Designed by Diane Stevenson / SNAP·HAUS GRAPHICS

Library of Congress Cataloging-in-Publication Data
The American promise : voices of a changing nation 1945–present /
edited by Milton Meltzer.
    p.   c.
  Includes bibliographical references.
  Summary: Describes major events in American history since the end
of World War II and discusses how they have influenced and shaped
American society.

ISBN 0-553-07020-7

  1. United States—Politics and government—1945- 2. United
States—Social conditions—195- 3. United States—Economic
conditions—1945- [1. United States—Politics and
government—1945- 2. United States—Social conditions—1945–
3. United States—Economic conditions—1945–] I. Meltzer, Milton,
1915–
E743.A568 1990
973.92—dc20   90-154
                                                                CIP
                                                                AC

Published simultaneously in the United States and Canada

Bantam Books are published by Bantam Books, a division of Bantam Doubleday
Dell Publishing Group, Inc. Its trademark, consisting of the words "Bantam
Books" and the portrayal of a rooster, is Registered in U.S. Patent and Trademark
Office and in other countries. Marca Registrada. Bantam Books, 666 Fifth Avenue,
New York, New York 10103.

PRINTED IN THE UNITED STATES OF AMERICA

RRD   0   9   8   7   6   5   4   3   2

CONTENTS

FOREWORD

"**A**merica was promises," the poet Archibald MacLeish wrote early in this century. Promises of the Founding Fathers when they declared, "We hold these truths to be self evident: that all men are created equal, that they are endowed by their Creator with certain unalienable rights, that among these are life, liberty, and the pursuit of happiness."

Ever since that revolutionary time Americans have struggled to fulfill the promise of freedom and equality and have found how hard it is to bring the dream of what *ought* to be into harmony with the practice of what *is*. This country was made—is made every day, even now—by millions of people who are pursuing the American dream.

★

The history we learn tells us much about the people who transformed the vast American continent and founded a nation out of a faith in freedom and democracy. The story goes far back in time to the migration of the Native Americans from Asia across the Bering Straits to the unpeopled wilderness of the Western Hemisphere. Whether or not we know specific details, we do know about the accounts of explorers and settlers, the building of colonies, the harsh labor to create farms and workshops, expanding frontiers, the American Revolution, the Civil War, industrialism, empire building, World War I . . .

We are aware of the events that happened long ago—but we know much less about the more recent past. The choices of Lincoln and FDR are familiar, but not those of Truman or Reagan. We've studied the Mexican War, and so it seems more real than the war in Korea or even the one in Vietnam.

The roots of historical change go deep into the past, but the life we live today is shaped powerfully by recent changes—by events occurring *since* World War II. Take a glance at how different things were around 1939, the year Hitler launched the war that engulfed the world. The United States was still stagnating in the Great Depression that had begun ten years before, with many millions still jobless. Only about one in seven young people went to college. African Americans north and south suffered vicious discrimination and segregation. Women were raised to marry, have children, and tend to the home. To have a career as well as a husband was not the thing to do. Very few women rose in the business world or went to professional schools to become lawyers, doctors, scientists, architects.

Fifty years ago it was the radio and the movies that people turned to for entertainment; no TV, no VCRs. As for music, the sound of rock and roll was not common.

It's a very different world today. How was it changed?

This book explores the major developments since World War II and discusses what they mean for us now. But it is not a chronological history of the usual kind. Instead, it is arranged by themes. The Cold War, the civil rights movement, the women's rights movement, the youth revolt, Vietnam, technology, and ecology are all issues that cannot be neatly packaged by the decade, or by presidential administrations; they spread out over many years. So in this book they are treated as a coherent whole.

Nor is this a narrative history. Instead, the book tries to explain the changes in American life through the personal experiences of the men and women who lived them. In their own words—through letters, diaries, memoirs, poems, speeches, songs, oral history interviews, newspaper reports, testimony given at public hearings—people tell their story. Some are leaders; many more are from the rank and file because this direct expression places you, the reader, at the heart of human experience that helped change the United States.

Each chapter opens with background for the theme it takes up, and a note sets the stage for each voice you hear. Cuts in the documents are indicated by ellipses (. . .). The source of each document is given at its end. The index will enable you to locate people, events, and topics.

C H A P T E R ★ 1

The underwater atomic blast in Bikini lagoon in 1946 produced a giant mushroom-shaped cloud formation moments after the explosion. The dark hole on the right side of the water column marks the approximate position of the battleship *Arkansas*, which was sunk by the blast. (WIDE WORLD PHOTOS)

A Bomb Explodes, a Trial Begins

★   ★   ★

The first atomic bomb was dropped by an American airplane over Hiroshima, Japan, on August 6, 1945, and its blast and fire devastated the city. Three days later a second atomic bomb fell upon Nagasaki. The two nuclear blasts killed two hundred thousand people. (WIDE WORLD PHOTOS)

Leaders of Nazi Germany in the courtroom at Nuremberg listening to testimony of the criminal charges against them. The trial, conducted before an international military tribunal in 1945–46, ended in death sentences for twelve of the defendants. (WIDE WORLD PHOTOS)

In August 1945 atomic bombs dropped by planes of the American Air Force exploded over Hiroshima and Nagasaki. Some two hundred thousand men, women, and children of those Japanese cities died of incineration and radiation. It marked the end of World War II and the beginning of the atomic age, certainly one of the most significant turns in world history.

At the time, America had a monopoly of atomic power. Some

claim that the bomb was used to force Japan to surrender at once, so that fewer American lives would be lost. Others say that the bombing was unnecessary: the Japanese were about to surrender, and the bomb was dropped instead to intimidate the Russians—our allies in the war—and gain diplomatic dominance over them in the postwar years.

Whatever the case, the horrifying threat of nuclear war has shadowed the world ever since. Soon the Soviet Union developed a nuclear arsenal, and so did a number of other countries. By 1988 the United States alone had stockpiled 25,000 nuclear warheads, enough firepower to wipe out the earth several times over. Roughly the same is true of the Russians' power to blast the globe to bits.

Danger of this magnitude is hard to imagine. To make it more real to the American citizen, Dr. Howard H. Hiatt of Harvard University tells what the effect of a nuclear explosion over New York would be. He based his scenario on materials prepared by the U.S. Arms Control and Disarmament Agency. He assumes a million-ton bomb is dropped on the city. While that bomb is fifty times more powerful than the bomb dropped on Hiroshima, it is far less destructive than the latest nuclear weapons. And while his imagined attack involves the explosion of a single bomb, the military planners all say that it is far more likely that many bombs would be used in an attack:

New York City's trial by nuclear attack begins with the detonation of a one-million ton air burst bomb 6,500 feet above the Empire State Building. The area of total destruction, the circle within which even the most heavily reinforced concrete structures do not survive, has a radius of 1.5 miles. That circle extends from the Brooklyn Bridge to Central Park Lake and from Long Island City to Hoboken. Included within it are the Empire State Building, Lincoln Center, the Stock Exchange. And within this circle, almost all of the population is killed.

At a distance of three miles from the center of the blast . . .

dissent. Resistance leaders such as Dr. Benjamin Spock and Rev. William Sloane Coffin were prosecuted and some of them jailed. Two brothers—the Catholic priests Philip and Daniel Berrigan— were imprisoned for burning draft board records in Catonsville, Maryland. Father Philip describes his prison experiences at Allenwood, Pennsylvania, in an interview from which these passages are taken:

Q. You are the first Catholic priest in this country to go to jail as a political prisoner. What does jail mean to you, and what were your first impressions inside a federal penitentiary?

A. I conceive of jail directly in terms of resistance—that is, how do you embarrass the Establishment, how do you shame them, how do you keep them off balance, how do you continue to bring to light the principles and issues that guide you in a time of grave national crisis? I see jail as an effective part of nonviolent tactics, which really do present alternatives to all sorts of people, and ought to be made policy. The big question, of course, is: How do you refashion this society? How do you bring its power to term, in a human fashion, before it destroys itself?

Q. What was a typical day at Allenwood like? At what time would you wake up?

A. The first buzzer would go off at six-thirty. And some men would immediately get up, go and get shaved, and very quickly get cleaned up and go to breakfast. Some would not eat breakfast; they would sleep until seven-thirty. That's optional, if you want to do it. Others would kind of straggle out between seven and seven-thirty. I hadn't been there more than two weeks before the chaplain over at the main penitentiary got me permission to say a private mass down at the chapel, which was on the lower end of the reservation, about a mile away. It was an old Protestant church that was used for both Protestant and Catholic services . . . I felt very, very deeply, too, the fact that nobody was allowed to worship with me. Later on, I'd go about every other day. And on Sundays I'd worship with the prisoners.

Q. Any restrictions on talking?

A. No restrictions on talking whatsoever. And a man who was really interested in meeting everyone and creating friendships can just rotate every meal, and meet new people every meal. There was a high degree of clique atmosphere there, some people always sitting with one another. But if you were really interested, you could get to know the whole prison population in the space of two to three months, just by doing a little thinking, and by going to their tables. . . .

Q. Was there any opportunity in the evenings for people to get together for common recreation, and was that time available for any kind of group discussion or study? Or was that reserved just for weekends or for time off when you wouldn't normally be working?

A. No, there was a great deal of that going on in the evening. Soon after I arrived there, through the acquaintances I had with the antiwar people especially, and also with a larger representation within the community, it became very apparent to me that there wasn't much moral and intellectual formation going on there, and that there was really a lot of fragmentation within the draft-resister community. So we talked a great deal about it, and finally agreed to meet.

So, along with some of the Catholic Worker people that I knew well, we started in, and slowly the group built up to about fifteen men. Some weeks we would have as many as two meetings, rather long and sustained sessions that would run perhaps three hours. This was really quite a feat and perhaps it indicates the level of interest that was being mobilized. Because these guys would come in very tired from the farm, kind of exhausted, and yet would stick around in a broiling room in one of the dormitories for a meeting that would run that long. Our view was, by and large, that the community ought to be an inclusive one, because it ought to be reaching out to the other communities in the prison—the Jewish community, the veterans' bunch that was around, the

Italian ethnic group (including the Mafia), the black community, and then the poor white community, mostly from the Appalachian area. We ought to be reaching all of them; that was one concern. In addition, we ought to be preparing ourselves for the time when we would be released from jail, so that we could be of use to the country and mankind. We tried to organize the meetings along these lines: how we could better serve the Allenwood community, in addition to that, how we could better prepare ourselves for life after jail. . . .

Q. Did these people see resistance as a personal thing, or more as a challenge to the conscience of the community?

A. You have to understand that people had gone into resistance for a vast variety of both personal and public reasons. There was a Jehovah's Witnesses community there, for example. They were more or less exclusive, in the sense that three times a week, a minimum, they would meet by themselves for prayer, for discussion, for group reading, and a variety of other activities that were part of their modus operandi there. They even took their recreation mostly together. They weren't approached, because it was known that they wouldn't respond. This is not to denigrate them; they simply were not political people. Of course, as a kind of thematic pattern for their lives, they were anti-government, whatever the government might be. . . .

But with the conventional resisters you would run into a guy—I remember one from Long Island—who wasn't interested in anything but returning to normalcy, as he viewed it, he just didn't want to be involved in killing. . . .

And there would be others who would say, well, jail is a completely useless process. We want to experience it and understand it, since we are here, but after that we would take measures to get out, meaning anything from accepting parole into the Army to full cooperation with the system in order to get a quick parole, a conventional parole.

In addition, there were some who were being radicalized

more and more all the time. I remember one Harvard student, a remarkable young man who had worked in the [Eugene] McCarthy campaign in a sustained fashion all through the summer of 1968 in the New England area, and he'd done it at great sacrifice to himself. He needed to earn money, and yet he felt himself compelled to pursue this political tack. But he saw the failure of everything that McCarthy stood for, and he felt that American politics as they had become institutionalized had no room at all for a man like Gene McCarthy, and that he could not be successful. This student's exposure at Allenwood corroborated his view, and he became more radicalized and even revolutionary while he was there, and I am sure is pursuing the same direction now, content with the role he was pursuing in jail and seeing a value in it. So, there were all sorts of viewpoints operating as to why people had come to Allenwood, what they should do while they were there, and what they ought to prepare themselves for later on.

From Philip Berrigan, *Prison Journals of
***A Priest Revolutionary,* Holt, 1970**

When America stumbled into Vietnam, it was following Cold War dogma: prevent the "loss" of any country to communism. The enormous cost became clearer by the end of that long war. But the piling up of nuclear weapons did not cease. People who feared a nuclear holocaust would be the inevitable outcome organized in small local groups—like Silo Plowshares—to try to call public attention to a policy they considered insane. Jean Gump, a grandmother and a mother of twelve, lived in Chicago, where she was active in church and community work. On Good Friday, 1986, she was arrested along with four other Catholics for an action she tells about:

We commemorated the crucifixion near Holden, Missouri. We hung a banner on the outside of the chain-link fence that read: SWORDS INTO PLOWSHARES, AN ACT OF HEALING.

Isaiah 2, from Scriptures: We will pound our swords into plow-shares and we will study war no more.

It's a Minuteman II silo, a first-strike weapon. There are 150 of these missiles. If one of these missiles were to leave the ground, it would decimate an area of seventy-two miles. And all the children and others. We wanted to make this weapon inoperable. We succeeded.

We carried three hammers, a wire-clipper, three baby bottles with our blood, papers with an indictment against the Christian church for its complicity. Ken Ripito, who is twenty-three, and Ken Moreland, who is twenty-five, went with me. The other two went to another silo about five miles away.

It is going to be the citizens that will have to eliminate these weapons. They were built by human hands. People are frightened of them, yet view them as our Gods of Metal. It is a chain-link fence with barbed wire on top. We have become so accustomed to these monstrosities that there are no guards. It is nondescript. If you were passing it on the road, you would see this fence. The silo itself is maybe a foot or two out of the earth. . . .

To get through the fence, we used a wire clipper. . . . Once we were in, I proceeded to use the blood and I made a cross on top of the silo. Underneath, I wrote the words, in black spray paint: DISARM AND LIVE.

We sat down and waited in prayer. We thanked God, first of all, that we were alive. We expected a helicopter to come over and kill us terrorists. We thanked God for our successful dismantling, more or less, of this weapon. We assumed the responsibility for our actions and we waited to be apprehended.

About forty minutes later, the soldiers arrived in an armored vehicle. There was a machine-gun turret at the top. The commander used a megaphone and said, "Will all the personnel on top of the silo please leave the premises with your hands raised?" So all of us personnel (laughs) left the silo. . . .

They put the men up against the fence in a spread-eagle position. They asked the female—myself—to "take ten steps and stand with your hands raised." I did it for a few minutes and my fingers were beginning to tingle. I put my hands down. The soldier said, "You must put your hands up." I said, "No, I have a little funny circulation." He said, "You must put your hands up." I said, "Shoot me." He chose not to, which I thought was good.

I said, "I'll compromise with you, I will raise my hands for five minutes and I will put them down for five minutes." He said, "You can't put them down." I said, "But I will." It was hysterical.

I wanted to turn around to see if my friends were being maltreated. The soldier who had his gun aimed at me said, "You can't turn around." I did. I was watching them try to put handcuffs on the two men. I have been arrested in Chicago. I've seen an efficient police force put handcuffs on people in two seconds. It must have taken these soldiers fifteen minutes. I had to tell them they were doing it wrong. With my suggestions, they finally did it right.

There was a big discussion about what to do with the female suspect. Apparently they weren't allowed to frisk a female suspect. I was kind of wondering what they were going to do with me. They asked me to remove my coat, which I did. He said, "Throw it ten feet over here." I said, "I'll never make it, but I'll do the best I can."

They took things out of my pocket and put them on the ground. One of the items was a handkerchief. I said, "It's getting a little chilly, I think I'm getting a cold and a runny nose. I will have to get my handkerchief." It was about three feet away. The soldier said, "Don't you dare move." I said, "I'm going to get this handkerchief and I'm going to blow my nose." I did that and put the handkerchief in my pocket. The soldier said, "You have to leave your handkerchief over here." I said, "All right. But if my nose should run again, I'll go over there and I will get my handkerchief and I will blow my nose." At this point, the poor soldier looked sort of crestfallen. He was about the age of my youngest child.

By this time, the area was filled with about eight automobiles. FBI, local sheriffs, and so on. They took us into this armored vehicle. On its right-hand side was a big sign: PEACEKEEPER. I said, "Young man, have an opportunity to read Orwell's *1984*." He said, "I'm not allowed to talk to you." I said, "I'll talk to you, then." He said, "If I had my uniform off, we could talk." I said, "Maybe we'll meet and have coffee someday . . ."

At the Federal Building in Kansas City, where we were taken, I was asleep on the bench. A nice young man joined me: "We might be able to negotiate something to get you out on bail." I said, "Young man, there's no way I'd pay a nickel for bail money. You're wasting your time." Darla, my co-cellmate, she's twenty-two, agreed also not to answer.

The judge said he'd like to let us out on a $5,000 bond, with our signature. We'd not commit any crimes between now and the arraignment date. John Volpe said, "I don't really know if I can, because there are a lot of silos out there."

My children knew nothing about this. Mother's doing her thing, is what they always say. As I leave the house, they often say, "Don't get arrested, ma." I'd been arrested five other times for civil disobedience.

I felt peace marching was fine, but what we needed was a freeze group. After campaigning in Morton Grove, we had a referendum. Five thousand voted for the freeze, two thousand against.

When I came back from Kansas City on Easter Sunday morning, the children had learned about it. There were tears between times of much laughter. They were supportive, though it's an imposition on their lives.

My one daughter graduates from the University of California. I will not be there. My other daughter is getting married. I will not be there. I want more than anything in the world to be there. These are my children and I love them. But if they're going to have a world, we have to stop this madness. I think they understand that as much as I want to be with them and with my loving husband—He wasn't with me on this at first, but now he's all the way.

About three weeks ago, I had asked for certain things to be done. I wanted the power of attorney for all our property to be in his hands. As he was going out the door, he said, "Jean, you're planning to die, aren't you?" It startled me because I'd been thinking about that. I thought it was something that could happen. Hearing him say it made it very real. I said, "Yeah, Joe." So we took up our lives again and our love affair has never been nicer.

My mother was a person that believed, I mean really believed, in justice. Maybe it came from her. When the kids were little, I always said, "Don't ever look to the next guy to effect change. Do it yourself." . . .

What I did on Good Friday in Holden, Missouri, is only the expression of my Christianity. This is God's world, okay? We are stewards of the earth. I think we're rather bad stewards.

You know, I have never been so hopeful. If I can change my way of thinking, anybody can. I don't want to be singled out as anybody special, because I'm not. We have got to have a future for our children and we've got to make some sacrifices for it, okay?

Call it a legacy, if you want to. What else is there? My grandchild, I want to offer him a life, that's all. We all had a crack at it, so I think it's fair that this generation should.

From Studs Terkel, *The Great Divide: Second Thoughts on the American Dream*, Pantheon, 1988

Jean Gump was sentenced to eight years (later reduced to six) in a federal penitentiary on the charge of conspiracy and destroying public property.

Sit-ins were a tactic used to break the back of segregation. Black students at North Carolina Agricultural and Technical College in Greensboro sat in at a Woolworth's lunch counter demanding to be served with white people. (WIDE WORLD PHOTOS)

Freedom Now!

The Struggle for

Civil Rights

★ ★ ★

When a federal court in 1957 ordered Central High School in Little Rock, Arkansas, to admit nine black students, racists tried to block their entrance. The state militia and an army mobilized by the federal government were on the scene to guarantee the students' safe admission. (WIDE WORLD PHOTOS)

Martin Luther King, Jr., addressed a crowd of thousands in front of the Lincoln Memorial at the 1963 March on Washington. (WIDE WORLD PHOTOS)

mericans fought in World War I under the slogan "Make the World Safe for Democracy"—but that world did not include the African American. In World War II the aim was to defeat Japan and Germany—the totalitarian aggressors. But even dur-

ing such a war to restore freedom and democracy, the American armed forces remained segregated and discrimination was common in the defense industries. It took mass action—the threat of a march on Washington organized by black leaders—before President Roosevelt issued Executive Order 8802 in 1941. It banned discrimination in hiring in defense industries or in government "because of race, creed, color, or national origin."

The agency set up to carry out this fair employment order began programs to better the economic position of blacks. But it was only a beginning. Step by step after the war the National Association for the Advancement of Colored People (NAACP) carried the fight for the franchise and for equal educational opportunity through the courts. At last, over ninety years after Emancipation, the basic rights of democracy for all were recognized. On May 17, 1954, the U.S. Supreme Court unanimously ruled that racial segregation in the public schools must be ended.

But resistance to the court's ruling sprang up overnight. Refusal to comply with the law took many forms, from doing nothing about it to bombings and riots in dozens of cities across the country.

Early in the fight Ruby Hurley came to Birmingham to open the first permanent NAACP office in the South. Here she tells what her life as a black organizer was like:

Every time I picked up the telephone it was a threatening call, and when I'd go home, I never knew whether it was going to be a bomb. . . . I couldn't eat, and days I'd go without food because I just could not eat in Jim Crow places. The only way I could get to a lot of places to fight for civil rights was by bus, and the bus stops, the places to eat, were all segregated, and I was not going to eat in a segregated place. So if I ran out of Hershey bars, then I didn't eat until I got someplace where I could be fed. Many times I'd have to ride all day or all morning in order to speak in the afternoon and then ride the rest of the night to get back home because there was no place for me to sleep. And that would mean ofttimes almost twenty-four hours when I didn't have anything to eat.

This was segregation. . . . I listen to young folks nowadays talking about old folks "taking it." They don't know how we didn't take it. There were those who died rather than take it, and there were those who suffered much more than I did who didn't take it, because I could get out every so often and go to New York and let off steam up there. I could go to Washington and let off steam up there. But there were people who lived under this hammer all the time, and who owned property and never knew when their property was gonna be taken away, or when their lives were going to be taken. . . . Much is said about what happened in the 1960s, but to me the fifties were much worse than the sixties. When I was out there by myself, for instance, there were no TV cameras with me to give me any protection. There were no reporters traveling with me to give me protection, because when the eye of the press or the eye of the camera was on the situation, it was different. . . .

I had to be very defensive, very careful about what I said, what I did, with whom I was seen. Efforts were made to entrap me sexually. All kinds of tricks were used, but . . . I have an ingrained ability to defend myself against anything that I think is wrong. So I was able to. . . .

But it was a challenge, and I always emphasize, but for the grace of God, I couldn't have done it, because there were days when if I'd had any sense, I'da been scared. But I never let myself. I didn't get scared . . . I was mad. . . . When I'd go downtown to buy clothes, I had to do battle about being recognized. I started a fight in Birmingham—the use of courtesy titles. I refused to spend my money and let some clerk that didn't have an eighth-grade education call me Ruby and she'd never seen me before in my life. Those are the kinds of things that took their toll inwardly, though I was able to, I think, effect at least a climate for some change. I think young people need to know, and some older people need to know, that it didn't all begin in 1960.

From Howell Raines, *My Soul Is Rested: Movement Days in the Deep South Remembered*, Putnam, 1977

After a court order was imposed on them in the fall of 1957, the school authorities in Little Rock, Arkansas, admitted nine black students to the all-white Central High School. White supremacists did their violent best to block the move toward integration. One of the nine boys and girls were Elizabeth Eckford. She tells of her feelings that first day when she was to enter Central High:

Before I left home Mother called us into the living room. She said we should have a word of prayer. Then I caught the bus and got off a block from the school. I saw a large crowd of people standing across the street from the soldiers guarding Central. As I walked on, the crowd suddenly got very quiet. Superintendent Blossom had told us to enter by the front door. I looked at all the people and thought, "Maybe I will be safer if I walk down the block to the front entrance behind the guards."

At the corner I tried to pass through the long line of guards around the school so as to enter the grounds behind them. One of the guards pointed across the street. So I pointed in the same direction and asked whether he meant for me to cross the street and walk down. He nodded "yes." So, I walked across the street conscious of the crowd that stood there, but they moved away from me.

For a moment all I could hear was the shuffling of their feet. Then someone shouted, "Here she comes, get ready!" I moved away from the crowd on the sidewalk and into the street. If the mob came at me I could then cross back over so the guards could protect me.

The crowd moved in closer and then began to follow me, calling me names. I still wasn't afraid. Just a little bit nervous. Then my knees started to shake all of a sudden and I wondered whether I could make it to the center entrance a block away. It was the longest block I ever walked in my whole life.

Even so, I still wasn't too scared because all the time I kept thinking that the guards would protect me. . . .

I stood looking at the school—it looked so big! Just then the guards let some white students go through.

The crowd was quiet. I guess they were waiting to see what was going to happen. When I was able to steady my knees, I walked up to the guard who had let the white students in. He too didn't move. When I tried to squeeze past him, he raised his bayonet and then the other guards closed in and they raised their bayonets.

They glared at me with a mean look and I was very frightened and didn't know what to do. I turned around and the crowd came toward me.

They moved closer and closer. Somebody started yelling, "Lynch her! Lynch her!"

I tried to see a friendly face somewhere in the mob—someone who maybe would help. I looked into the face of an old woman and it seemed a kind face, but when I looked at her again, she spat on me.

They came closer, shouting, "No nigger bitch is going to get in our school. Get out of here!"

I turned back to the guards but their faces told me I wouldn't get help from them. Then I looked down the block and saw a bench at the bus stop. I thought, "If I can only get there I will be safe." I don't know why the bench seemed a safe place to me, but I started walking toward it. I tried to close my mind to what they were shouting, and kept saying to myself, "If I can only make it to the bench I will be safe."

When I finally got there, I don't think I could have gone another step. I sat down and the mob crowded up and began shouting all over again. Someone hollered, "Drag her over to this tree! Let's take care of the nigger." Just then a white man sat down beside me, put his arm around me and patted my shoulder. He raised my chin and said, "Don't let them see you cry."

Then a white lady—she was very nice—she came over to me on the bench. She spoke to me but I don't remember what she said. She put me on the bus and sat next to me. She asked my name and tried to talk to me but I don't think I answered.

I can't remember much about the bus ride, but the next thing I remember I was standing in front of the School for the Blind where Mother works.

From Daisy Bates, *The Long Shadow of Little Rock*, McKay, 1962

In the end, it took an army division plus the state militia to ensure that these children might safely enter Central High. Another step toward breaking the back of segregation began with sit-ins. What they were, and how they got started, is told by Franklin McCain, then a student at all-black North Carolina A&T College in Greensboro. He and his three closest friends, Ezell Blair, Jr., David Richmond, and Joseph McNeill, talked about justice and how poorly this America fulfilled its promise. Why, for instance, couldn't blacks go into any eating place and be served together with whites? Their many bull sessions got around to a debate about what a moral man might do to remedy injustice:

The planning process was on a Sunday night, I remember it quite well. I think it was Joseph who said, "It's time that we take some action now. We've been getting together, and we've been, up to this point, still like most people who talk a lot but, in fact, make very little action." After selecting the technique, then we said, "Let's go down and just ask for service." It certainly wasn't titled a "sit-in" at that time. "Let's just go down to Woolworth's tomorrow and ask for service, and the tactic is going to be simply this: we'll just stay there." We never anticipated being served, certainly, the first day anyway. "We'll stay until we get served." And I think Ezell said, "Well, you know that might be weeks, that might be months, that might be never." And I think it was the consensus of the group, we said, "Well, that's just the chance we'll have to take."

What's likely to happen? Now, I think that that was a question that all of us asked ourselves. . . . What's going to happen once we sit down? Of course, nobody had the answers. Even your wildest imagination couldn't lead you to believe what would, in fact, happen.

Once getting there . . . we did make purchases of school supplies and took the patience and time to get receipts for our purchases, and Joseph and myself went over to the counter and asked to be served coffee and doughnuts. As anticipated, the reply was, "I'm sorry, we don't serve you here." And of course we said, "We just beg to disagree with you. We've in fact already been served; you've served us already and that's just not quite true." The attendant or waitress was a little bit dumbfounded, just didn't know what to say under circumstances like that. And we said, "We wonder why you'd invite us in to serve us at one counter and deny service at another. If this is a private club or private concern, then we believe you ought to sell membership cards and sell only to persons who have a membership card. If we don't have a card, then we'd know pretty well that we shouldn't come in or even attempt to come in." That didn't go over too well, simply because I don't really think she understood what we were talking about, and for the second reason, she had no logical response to a statement like that. And the only thing that an individual in her case or position could do is, of course, call the manager. Well, at this time, I think we were joined by Dave Richmond and Ezell Blair at the counter with us, after that dialogue . . .

At that point there was a policeman who had walked in off the street, who was pacing the aisle . . . behind us, where we were seated, with his club in his hand, just sort of knocking it in his hand, and just looking mean and red and a little bit upset and a little bit disgusted. And you had the feeling that he didn't know what the hell to do. You had the feeling that this is the first time that this big bad man with the gun and the club has been pushed in a corner, and he's got absolutely no defense, and the thing that's killing him more than anything else—he doesn't know what he can or what he cannot do. Usually his defense is offense, and we've provoked him, yes, but we haven't provoked him outwardly enough for him to resort to violence. And I think this is just killing him; you can see it all over him.

People in the store were—we got mixed reactions from people in the store. A couple of old ladies . . . came up to pat us on the back sort of and say, "Ah, you should have done it ten years ago. It's a good thing I think you're doing."

These were white ladies. And I think that was certainly some incentive for additional courage on the part of us. And the other thing that helped us psychologically quite a lot was seeing the policeman pace the aisle and not be able to do anything. I think that this probably gave us more strength, more encouragement, than anything else on that particular day, on day one . . .

There was virtually nothing that could move us, there was virtually nothing probably at that point that could really frighten us off. . . . If it's possible to know what it means to have your soul cleansed—I felt pretty clean at that time. I probably felt better on that day than I've ever felt in my life. . . .

Mr. Harris, who was the store manager, he was a fairly nice guy to talk to on that day. I think what he wanted to do more than anything else was to—initially—was to kill us with kindness, to say, "Fellas, you know this is just not the way we do business. Why don't you go on back to your campus? If you're just hungry, go downstairs," and that sort of thing.

We listened to him, paid him the courtesy of listening to what he had to say. We repeated our demands to him, and he ended up by saying, "Well, you know, I don't really set policy for this store.

The policy for serving you is set by corporate headquarters.'' And of course, we found out that that was just a cop out. Corporate headquarters said, ''No, it's up to local communities to set standards and set practices and that sort of thing, and whatever they do is all right with us. . . .''

The only reason we did leave is the store was closing. We knew, of course, we had to leave when the store was closing. We said to him, ''Well, we'll have plenty of time tomorrow, because we'll be back to see you.'' [Laughs] I don't think that went over too well. But by the time we were leaving, the store was just crowded with people from off the streets and on the streets. . . . As a matter of fact, there were so many people standin' in front of the store, we had to leave from the side entrance. . . .

From Howell Raines, *My Soul Is Rested*, Putnam, 1977

The students were following the principle of nonviolent resistance to injustice developed long before by the writer Henry David Thoreau. Thoreau went to jail in Concord, Massachusetts, in 1846 when he refused to pay his taxes in protest against a government that supported slavery. His method of civil disobedience was expanded to massive resistance in the great Montgomery bus boycott led by Rev. Martin Luther King, Jr., in 1955–56. The refusal to ride the buses forced the city to desegregate the system. The boycott was picked up throughout the country as the weapon that could bring about change. Here Dr. King states what he learned from the Montgomery experience:

The experience in Montgomery did more to clarify my thinking on the question of nonviolence than all of the books that I had read. As the days unfolded I became more and more convinced of the power of nonviolence. . . . Many issues I had not cleared up intellectually concerning nonviolence were now solved in the sphere of practical action. . . .

I do not want to give the impression that nonviolence will

work miracles overnight. Men are not easily moved from their mental ruts or purged of their prejudiced and irrational feelings. When the underprivileged demand freedom, the privileged first react with bitterness and resistance. Even when the demands are couched in nonviolent terms, the initial response is the same. I am sure that many of our white brothers in Montgomery and across the south are still bitter toward Negro leaders, even though these leaders sought to follow a way of love and nonviolence. So the nonviolent approach does not immediately change the heart of the oppressor. It first does something to the hearts and souls of those committed to it. It gives them new self-respect; it calls up resources of strength and courage that they did not know they had. Finally, it reaches the opponent and so stirs his conscience that reconciliation becomes a reality.

From Dr. Martin Luther King, Jr., "Pilgrimage to Non-Violence,"
The Christian Century, **April 13, 1960**

Woolworth's and hundreds of other stores were soon open to all races. In the years that followed, sit-ins desegregated beaches, swimming pools, hotels, restaurants, theaters, amusement parks. In the spring of 1961 the movement spread to transportation. Although the Supreme Court had ruled against segregated seating on interstate buses back in 1946, and in 1960 against segregated terminal facilities, the white South ignored the law. The Congress of Racial Equality (CORE) led by James Farmer informed federal government authorities and the major bus companies that blacks and whites together would travel to the South and deliberately violate segregation on buses and at the rest stops. They said their action would be absolutely nonviolent.

The Freedom Riders left Washington. The bus ride was peaceful until they reached Anniston, a center of Alabama's Ku Klux Klan. At the depot white men holding iron bars watched the bus pull in. The police held them back, but the Kluxers, as the Klansmen were called, caught up with the bus about six miles out of town. Hank Thomas, one of the Freedom Riders, describes what happened:

Igot real scared then. You know, I was thinking—I'm looking out the window there, and people are out there yelling and screaming. They just about broke every window out of the bus. . . . I really thought that that was going to be the end of me.

They shot the tires out, and the bus driver was forced to stop. . . . He got off, and man, he took off like a rabbit, and might well have. I couldn't very well blame him there. And we were trapped on the bus. They tried to board. Well, we did have two FBI men aboard the bus. All they were there to do was to observe and gather facts, but the crowd apparently recognized them as FBI men, and they did not try to hurt them.

It wasn't until the thing was shot on the bus and the bus caught afire that everything got out of control, and . . . when the bus was burning . . . panic did get ahold of me. Needless to say, I couldn't survive that burning bus. There was a possibility I could have survived the mob, but I was just so afraid of the mob that I was gonna stay on that bus. I mean, I just got that much afraid. . . . Somebody said, "Hey, the bus is gonna explode," because it had just gassed up, and so they started scattering then, and I guess that's the way we got off the bus. Otherwise, we probably all would have been succumbed by the smoke, and not being able to get off, probably would have been burned alive or burned on there anyway. That's the only time I was really, really afraid. . . .

The people at the hospital would not do anything for us. They would not. And I was saying, "You're doctors, you're medical personnel." They wouldn't. Governor Patterson got on statewide radio and said, "Any rioters in this state will not receive police protection." And then the crowd started forming outside the hospital, and the hospital told us to leave. And we said, "No, we're not going out there," and there we were. A caravan from Birmingham, about a fifteen-car caravan led by the Reverend Fred

Shuttlesworth, came up from Birmingham to get us out. Without police escort, but every one of those cars had a shotgun in it. And Fred Shuttlesworth had got on the radio and said . . . "I'm going to get my people." And apparently a hell of a lot of people believed in him. . . . And each one of 'em got out with their guns and everything and the state police were there, but I think they all realized that this was not a time to say anything because, I'm pretty sure, there would have been a lot of people killed.

And that's how we got back to Birmingham. . . . I think I was flown to New Orleans for medical treatment, because still they were afraid to let any of us go to the hospitals in Birmingham, and by that time—it was what, two days later—I was fairly all right. I had gotten most of the smoke out of my system.

From Howell Raines, *My Soul Is Rested*, Putnam, 1977

The savage resistance ended only when hundreds of federal marshals appeared. Changing tactics, local officials stopped arresting demonstrators for violating segregation ordinances. Instead, they tossed them into jail for disorderly conduct or creating a disturbance. To illustrate how the nonviolent movement was persecuted, here are some examples recorded over some eight weeks of 1961 in Mississippi alone:

August 15, Amite County: Robert Moses, Student Non-Violent Coordinating Committee (SNCC) registration worker, and three Negroes who had tried unsuccessfully to register in Liberty, were driving toward McComb when a county officer stopped them. He asked if Moses was the man "who's been trying to register our niggers." All were taken to court and Moses was arrested for "impeding an officer in the discharge of his duties," fined $50 and spent two days in jail.

August 22, Amite County: Robert Moses went to Liberty with three Negroes, who made an unsuccessful attempt to register. A block from the courthouse, Moses was attacked and beaten by

Billy Jack Caston, the sheriff's first cousin. Eight stitches were required to close a wound in Moses' head. Caston was acquitted of assault charges by an all-white jury before a justice of the peace.

August 26, McComb, Pike County: Hollis Watkins, 20, and Elmer Hayes, 20, SNCC workers, were arrested while staging a sit-in at the F. W. Woolworth store and charged with breach of the peace. They spent 36 days in jail.

August 27 and 29, McComb, Pike County: Five Negro students from a local high school were convicted of breach of the peace following a sit-in at a variety store and bus terminal. They were sentenced to a $400 fine each and eight months in jail. One of these students, a girl of 15, was turned over to juvenile authorities, released, subsequently rearrested, and sentenced to 12 months in a state school for delinquents.

August 30, McComb, Pike County: SNCC workers Brenda Travis, 16, Robert Talbert, 19, and Isaac Lewis, 20, staged a sit-in in the McComb terminal of the Greyhound bus lines. They were arrested on charges of breach of the peace and failure to obey a policeman's order to move on. They spent 30 days in jail.

September 5, Liberty, Amite County: Travis Britt, SNCC registration worker, was attacked and beaten by whites on the courthouse lawn. Britt was accompanied at the time by Robert Moses. Britt said one man hit him more than 20 times. The attackers drove away in a truck.

September 7, Tylertown, Walthall County: John Hardy, SNCC registration worker, took two Negroes to the county courthouse to register. The registrar told him he "wasn't registering voters" that day. When the three turned to leave, Registrar John Q. Wood took a pistol from his desk and struck Hardy over the head from behind. Hardy was arrested and charged with disturbing the peace.

September 25, Liberty, Amite County: Herbert Lee, a Negro who had been active in voter registration, was shot and killed by white state representative E. H. Hurst in downtown Liberty. No prosecution was undertaken, the authorities explaining that the representative had shot in self-defense.

October 4, McComb, Pike County: The five students who were arrested as a result of the August 29 sit-in in McComb returned to school, but were refused admittance. At that, 116 students walked out and paraded downtown to the city hall in protest. Police arrested the entire crowd, but later released all but 19, all of whom were 18 years old or older. They were charged with breach of the peace and contributing to the delinquency of minors and allowed to go free on bail totaling $3,700. At the trial on October 31, Judge Brumfield, finding the students guilty, and sentencing each to a $500 fine and six months in jail, said: "Some of you are local residents, some of you are outsiders. Those of you who are local residents are like sheep being led to the slaughter. If you continue to follow the advice of outside agitators, you will be like sheep and be slaughtered."

From *Mississippi Violence vs. Human Rights*, Committee for the Distribution of the Mississippi Story, Atlanta, 1963

Bernice Johnson Reagon was one of the original Freedom Singers in Albany, Georgia, where civil rights protests lasted from 1961 to 1965. Her father was a minister and she grew up in the church. When Reagon was arrested, she and the others began singing in jail. Their music transformed the singers and the movement. (Now Reagon sings with Sweet Honey in the Rock, the female group she founded which tours the country and makes recordings.) In this interview she tells what the music meant to the movement:

If you get together in a Black situation, you sing and, during that period, you would pray. If it's Black, that's what you were gonna do.

There is a kind of singing that happens in church that is really fervent, powerful singing. . . . Ordinarily you go to church and you sing but sometimes the congregation takes the roof off the building. Every mass meeting was like that. . . . And that level of expression, that level of cultural power present in an everyday situation, gave a more practical or functional meaning to the music than when it was sung in church on Sunday. The music actually was a group statement. If you look at the music and the words that came out of the Movement, you will find the analysis that the masses had about what they were doing.

One song that started out to be sung in Albany was, "Ain't gonna let nobody turn me 'round."

> *Ain't gonna let Pritchett turn me round,*
> *I'm on my way to freedom land.*
> *If you don't go, don't hinder me,*
> *Come and go with me to that land where I'm bound.*
> *There ain't nothing but peace in that land,*
> *Nothing but peace.*

There was a lady who sang that song who had a voice like thunder. She would sing it for about 30 minutes. She would also sing the song in church meetings on Sunday. The song in either place said—where I am is not where I'm staying. "Come and go with me to that land" had a kind of arrogance about being in motion. A lot of Black songs are like that, especially group ones. If you read the lyrics strictly you may miss the centering element, the thing that makes people chime in and really make it a powerful song. Singing voiced the basic position of movement, of taking action on your life.

It was also in the Movement that I heard a woman pray and heard the prayer for the first time. It was a standard prayer:

> *Lord, here come me, your meek and undone servant*
> *Knee-bent and body-bowed to the motherdust*
>   *of the earth.*
> *You know me and you know my condition.*
> *We're down here begging you to come and help us.*

We had just come back from a demonstration. The lines said, "We're down here—you know our condition. We need you." All those things became graphic for me. They were graphic in my everyday life but when I heard those prayers in a mass meeting, it was like a prayer of a whole people. Then I understood what in fact we (Black church) had been doing for a long time. The Movement released this material, songs and prayer, created by Black people, that made sense used in an everyday practical way and in a position of struggle. . . .

By the time of Albany, there was a tradition of singing in the Movement that came out of the sit-ins and the bus Freedom Riders. "We Shall Overcome" was already considered the theme song. Already there was a musical statement being made that paralleled all the other activities. As that body of music came through Albany, it was changed. You had old ladies leading freedom songs, backed by old ladies and old men who really knew what the songs were like before they'd gotten to the college campus or wherever else. Like the old song "Amen" which turned to "Freedom." That same song has been done for centuries in the Black church. You can put a harmony, 1–3–5, soprano-alto-tenor-bass, to that and get a tight choral sound. A SNCC worker would start to do "Amen" in Georgia and it would be taken over by the congregation who would sing it the way they always sang it. They were singing "Freedom" but they sang it in the same way they sang "Amen." That wouldn't be an arranged hymn. "Amen" is a Black traditional song and it's actually an upbeat song. Lots of songs changed like that.

When SNCC came to Albany, we were singing "We Shall Overcome," because in the church where we sang it on Sundays it was "I'll Overcome." . . . As far as you're concerned, you are singing the same song they're singing, even though it's different. By the time "We Shall Overcome" got to Albany it had become ritualized as the symbol of the Movement. They were doing it standing, holding hands. "We" was really important as a concern for the group. There were one or two other changes. We were doing it a little faster than they were doing it. We slowed it down a little bit—that's just the students in Albany and the SNCC workers—and by the time it got to a mass meeting, something else happened to it in terms of improvisation and slowing it down more. . . .

There were real class differences between the Black women in jail, and music had a lot to do with breaking down those things because there were several women in there who could lead songs, of different ages, and everybody would back everybody up. It was the first time I led songs and felt totally backed up by a group of Blacks. . . .

There was something about the Civil Rights Movement, where leaders were defined by their activism. Not by their age or their class, so within the Black community people began to look up to students, to ask students what should they do about x, y, and z, and follow the leadership of all sorts of different people based on what they perceived to be an integrity and commitment to struggle and stick with that particular struggle. . . .

There was a sense of power, in a place where you didn't feel you had any power. There was a sense of confronting things that terrified you, like jail, police, walking in the street—you know, a whole lot of Black folks couldn't even walk in the street in those places in the South. So you were saying in some basic way, "I will never again stay inside these boundaries."

From Dick Cluster, ed., *They Should Have Served*
That Cup of Coffee: Seven Radicals Remember the '60s,
South End Press, 1979

In 1963—the centennial of the Emancipation Proclamation— four black children were killed when a Birmingham church was bombed. Noting their deaths, I. F. Stone, a white political journalist working in Washington, wrote a piece he called "The Wasteland in the White Man's Heart":

It's not so much the killings as the lack of contrition. The morning after the Birmingham bombing, the Senate in its expansive fashion filled thirty-five pages of the Congressional Record with remarks on diverse matters before resuming debate on the nuclear test ban treaty. But the speeches on the bombing in Birmingham filled barely a single page. Of a hundred ordinarily loquacious Senators, only four felt moved to speak . . .

If four children had been killed in the bombing of a Berlin church by communists, the country would be on the verge of war. But when four Senators framed a resolution asking that the Sunday after the Birmingham bombing be set aside as a national day of mourning, they knew their fellow Senators too well even to introduce it. They sent it on to the White House where it was lost in the shuffle. Despite the formal expressions of regret, the sermons, the editorials and the marches, neither white America nor its leadership was really moved.

When Martin Luther King and six other Negro leaders finally saw the President four days after the bombing, it was to find that he had already appointed a two-man committee to represent him "personally" in Birmingham, but both men were white. This hardly set a precedent for bi-racial action. If Mr. Kennedy could take a judge off the Supreme Court to settle a labor dispute, he could have taken one of the country's two Negro judges off the Court of Appeals to dignify a mission of mediation. He might have insisted, for once, after so terrible a crime, on seeing white and Negro leaders together, instead of giving a separate audience four days later to a white delegation from Birmingham. It is as if, even in the White House, there are equal but separate facilities. . . .

When I was in Germany, I felt the empty wasteland of the German heart. I feel the same way about the hearts of my fellow white men in America, where the Negro is concerned. The good people there as here are in the minority and weak. Just as many Germans feel it was somehow the fault of the Jews that they got themselves cremated, so many whites here, North and South, feel

School for Retarded Children. Esperanza—Hope. We did everything to get the state to put up the money. And Bobby went to school for the first time in his life and made friends and looked forward to every day.

Some of the same crazy people we were warned against now said, Let's get a program started for adults. The state said there's no documentation of a need for a sheltered workshop in this area. So we knocked on every door in the neighborhood, looking for people physically or mentally handicapped. . . .

We hired someone at a minimal wage and opened shop with ·twelve people. We didn't know what we were doin', but we were doin' it. Within a week, the state was crawlin' all over us: You're not allowed. We said, We did it and we're not closin'. So they sat down, negotiated, and gave us $20,000. That was 1972. Today, this workshop has four residential centers and a baby center. And is $1.7 million. This all started because we had to get something for Bobby. . . .

In the sixties and early seventies, I viewed myself as a person who had to change something. I had to get the garbage picked up regularly or get rid of some principal or get a new school constructed. Now, evolution has brought me to saying: I have to change how people view themselves in the world. I have to get people to believe that they can in fact make the difference. If I can create the transition in the human being, the garbage and the school will get taken care of. We view ourselves more as people trained to develop people. Issues are only tools.

Think about the guy who works in a factory. He's on the assembly line. He's a nobody. He doesn't do the kind of work that's ever gonna get him recognition. Take that same person and he's a key leader in the parish or in a union. Suddenly that same man, who from Monday to Friday stands on the assembly line at General Motors and is nobody, is somebody over here. People look to him. He makes a difference and he knows it. He counts.

From Studs Terkel, *The Great Divide*, Pantheon, 1988

In the small town of Brewster, Massachusetts, a congregation of Unitarians made the First Parish Universalist Church a sanctuary for refugees from Central America. They did it after much debate about conscience and its obligations. In these same New England towns back in the 1850s people had defied the Fugitive Slave Law to give aid and shelter to runaway slaves. Now poor and persecuted peasants from the countries of Central America were crossing our borders illegally hoping for sanctuary in a free nation.

Rev. James A. Robinson tells us how and why his congregation came to this decision:

As the civil war is raging in Guatemala and El Salvador, the people in the church became aware of the large number of massacres and death squads and decided that they'd like our church to do something to help the victims of this situation. And then we became aware of the large number of refugees in the United States, particularly Salvadorans. . . . The fact is that these people are illegal aliens and not allowed any legal status in the United States. We had read that a large number of these people are deported back to El Salvador. . . . A significant number of them, maybe up to a quarter or a third of them, end up dead within several months. There are even some shoot-outs at the airport and this, according to our expert at the Unitarian Headquarters, is because these refugees would arrive back in their villages and the right-wing death squads would assume they must be guerrillas because they had been missing for some amount of time, and so they'd be assassinated quietly. And so we perceive the threat to these people's lives to be a real one—these people who are being deported. . . .

We became aware of a nationwide movement, which at that time had forty churches—none in New England—who were offering sanctuary to Salvadorans and Guatemalans, which meant that they would accept these refugees and care for them and help them find jobs. . . . So we decided to suggest to the congregation that we become a sanctuary site, and we went through some intense discussion with the church membership because the thought for many of them that the church would stand up and break the law was just more than they could bear. Church had meant to them a place to come to worship, and to stand up in that sort of sense really put us all in a lot of turmoil. After three weeks of intense discussions throughout the church, we decided to, in a sense, have a bit of a compromise. It was a unanimous vote to give a moral endorsement to any individuals in the church and to the Social Concerns Committee of the church to go ahead and declare Sanctuary. So then we set up a sanctuary site and we let it be known.

First the newspapers all flocked in and called up the INS (Immigration and Naturalization Service), and they told them we were breaking the law and we would go to jail for five years and all this stuff. Essentially the government, the INS, had said that "Yes, you're breaking the law, but we don't plan to prosecute any churches at this time." That basically was the answer we got. . . .

We go around to a lot of other churches now and basically we find a lot of interest, but everybody says, "Oh, we could never do this in our church." And the reason for all the hesitation is that there was, and there is, a danger of splitting churches on this kind of issue. In other words, half the people say, "I vote against it" and a quarter of the people are saying, "If you pass this, I'm going to leave the church." And if the church splits like that, then my job is in jeopardy. . . . So there are real risks, and I had some sleepless nights over those risks because I happen to like my job. . . .

I think what we're talking about is what I'd call civil disobedience. And that is where an individual makes a choice, a conscious choice, to disobey a law because they feel there's a higher moral order at stake and that they have to be willing to accept the consequences of that choice, if there be consequences. That to me is what principled dissent or civil disobedience is. There should be enough principled dissent to keep the moral order moving forward, but not so much that chaos results. . . . I would be opposed to violent revolution. There shouldn't be restrictions on people's opinions. Oh, certainly not. There should be a free marketplace of ideas. . . .

I think it's a part of American history. I mean, we were a sanctuary for persecuted religious groups in our beginning and we've been a sanctuary for different immigrant groups who fled either economic hardship or actual persecution. Sanctuary has been a part of our heritage. The Statue of Liberty is supposed to be a symbol of sanctuary for the poor and huddled masses. Now she's getting her face lifted with this credit card thing and everything. I mean, it's like the Establishment has taken over our huddled masses. We've had a lot of people call us an underground railroad because some of the refugees end up in Canada with political asylum and we're a stopping ground for them. I'd say we have somewhere between ten and fifteen new members in the church because of the stand we took. And some of those are active in the project. . . .

I think the general public has looked at what we've done and said, ''My God, they are giving humanitarian help to some suffering human beings and somehow that's right.''

From John Langston Gwaltney, *The Dissenters:*
Voices from Contemporary America, **Random House, 1986**

And what about the very first immigrants, the Native Americans? They have been harried by continuing violations of treaty commitments made by the whites who invaded their territory from the time of Columbus on. Brutal economic pressures have made their history a struggle for survival.

Vine Deloria, Jr., a Sioux Indian, is best known for his book Custer Died for Your Sins: An Indian Manifesto. *At forty-five, he was teaching political science at the University of Arizona when he gave this interview:*

I grew up on the Pine Ridge reservation in South Dakota. It was about thirty-five miles from Wounded Knee. The town was about four blocks long and three blocks wide, off Main Street. It was really only about two blocks of buildings. I remember before they put the pavement in. The roads were just cow pastures. When it rained, you were there for a couple of days. Very few whites lived there.

I went to grade school, half white and half mixed-blood Indians. They taught us Rudyard Kipling's world view. It was a simplistic theory that societies marched toward industry and that science was doing good for us. . . . There was a heavy overtone of the old British colonial attitude. Nothing about the slaves. Minority history just didn't exist. The world somehow is the garden of the white people, and everybody else kind of fits in someplace. And it's not demeaning to fit in, 'cause that's the way God wants it. You're not being put down. Western civilization's finding a place for you. . . .

My father was an Episcopal missionary on the reservation. His father was too. I suppose our family was one of the first to move from the old ways to the white man's ways. It was a weird situation, schizophrenic. My family had been religious leaders before they'd become Christians. The old Indian religion. I was not just a minister's son. Mine was a long family tradition of medicine men. People came to my father for all sorts of things. He knew all kinds of medicine songs and stories.

He held on to the two cultures without much conflict until the late sixties. The civil rights movement turned him off. The church put tremendous pressure on the Indians to integrate. He said: "We don't have to. We can be what we are without getting into the melting pot.''. . .

Maybe my generation is the last one that was affected by Indian values. I'm forty-five. Now I see people, about eight years younger, going to a meeting and starting to dominate things right away. When I was five and six, older relatives shushed me up at meetings because no one should talk unless the oldest person talks. People of my age still feel these social constraints. If you move eight years down, you find people who've grown up in postwar brashness. The hustler. The further down you move, the worse it gets. The younger people have taken the rat race as the real thing. It's a thing in their heads. In my generation, it was a thing in the heart. . . .

Maybe the American Dream is in the past, understanding who you are instead of looking to the future: What are you going to be? 'Cause we've kind of reached the future. I'm not just talking about nostalgia. I'm talking about finding familiar guideposts. . . .

I think there will emerge a group of people, not a large percentage, who will somehow find a way to live meaningful lives. For the vast majority, it will be increased drudgery, with emotions sapped by institutional confines. A grayness. A lot of people are fighting back.

Somewhere, America stalled in perpetual adolescence. But I don't really despair. You can't despair that you have to grow up.

From Studs Terkel, *American Dreams*, Pantheon, 1980

Concerned citizens in Tampa, Florida, provided a homeless family of seven with a place to stay and food. The family had lived in a picnic shelter before help was offered. (WIDE WORLD PHOTOS)

Plenty—and Poverty:

A Declining Economy

★   ★   ★

As the end of the twentieth century neared, Americans began to worry about their future as the world's number one power. Only forty years before, the United States had been the unchallenged leader in the global economy. It was the industrial and financial center of the world. Its inventions, its science, its technology were envied by all.

Yet by the 1980s gloomy forecasts of America's declining power and authority became common talk. Other nations and regions competing for industrial and trade leadership were now outstripping the United States. American manufacturing in several sectors gave in to foreign competition. From a manufacturing country, America declined into a service economy.

Though the wealth of the top few percent swelled ever larger, the income of the middle and bottom layers shrank. But signs of stubborn pockets of poverty within the generally prosperous economy of postwar America had been detected much earlier. In 1962 a book appeared that blew away the illusory hope that there might be no poor. It was called The Other America—the America of the poor. Written by Michael Harrington, it was one of those powerful pieces of social literature that rouse a whole nation to a challenge it must meet. Like Uncle Tom's Cabin, like The Jungle, like The Feminine Mystique, it pried open closed minds and prodded the government to act to remedy a terrible wrong. In these passages from his first chapter, Harrington takes the blinders off the public eye:

There is a familiar America. It is celebrated in speeches and advertised on television and in the magazines. It has the highest mass standard of living the world has ever known.

In the 1950's this America worried about itself, yet even its anxieties were products of abundance. The title of a brilliant book was widely misinterpreted, and the familiar America be-public that is being asked to assume the risks that the insect controllers calculate. The public must decide whether it wishes to continue on the present road, and it can do so only when in full possession of the facts. In the words of Jean Rostand, "The obligation to endure gives us the right to know."

From Rachel Carson, *Silent Spring*, Houghton Mifflin, 1962

The public concern roused by Carson's book led to the formation of many citizen's groups determined to press government to act in defense of the environment. In 1970 Congress passed and President Nixon signed the National Environmental Policy Act and established the Environmental Protection Agency. Its aim was to bring together agencies dealing with water quality, air pollution, and waste disposal. It also set standards for the disposal of nuclear waste and regulated the use of pesticides.

But almost twenty years after Silent Spring *nowhere near enough was being done to carry out the mandate of Congress. Ralph Nader, the noted citizens' advocate, argued that chemical poisons from toxic wastes were putting the health of all Americans at great risk and that the chemical industry was ignoring its responsibility to protect the public. With two of his associates Nader published the evidence in a book called* Who's Poisoning America: Corporate Polluters and Their Victims in the Chemical Age. *These are excerpts from it:*

Chemical waste dumps number in the tens of thousands throughout this country. Additional volumes of waste have been illegally thrown into sewers, ravines and parking lots, or have been abandoned in urban warehouses. Millions of Americans are drinking water contaminated with toxic substances or finding water sources quarantined by health authorities. Residues of chemical pesticides pervade the food supply. Thousands of new chemical compounds are entering the human environment each year, and each year the evidence grows of even greater danger.

This epidemic of chemical violence spilling across the land and waters of America provokes a new patriotism: to stop the poisoning of the country. It invites a new kind of neighborhood unity: to defend the community, the children and those yet unborn. It highlights the severe deficiencies in our laws, in the flow of information and in the response of our public officials. It reflects a destruction of civilized standards by corporate executives. . . . Although it usually avoids immediate pain it silently generates future devastation.

But the future is now, and there may be worse to come. The names "Love Canal," "Kepone," "West Valley," "Reserve Mining," "2, 4, 5-T," "PBB," and "PCB" will be remembered for early tragedies in America's long struggle for self-defense against callous internal chemical warfare. The names of the companies responsible for these toxic spills and toxic dumps are seen on television or in the press. However, almost no one knows the names of the managers behind the company images.

In contrast, the victims know one another's names. Ask the farmers whose land and kin were contaminated with a fire retardant called PBB that was carelessly mixed with feed grain sold in Michigan. How well the families at Love Canal came to know each other as they learned that they themselves were going to have to impose accountability. . . .

Information about the effects of new substances should be made available to the public before the food chain and drinking water are contaminated. People need to know that many industrial materials are not necessary for a prosperous standard of living. Alternatives to these hazardous chemicals have been found—but, as a rule, only after an environmental disaster prompted a reevaluation.

PCB, PBB and Kepone are no longer produced, and most uses of 2, 4, 5-T are suspended; industry has adapted, agriculture continues. Reserve Mining Company could have disposed of its daily wastes onshore as did its smaller competitors nearby. And

Hooker Chemical Company certainly knew how to contain its myriad of chemicals more safely.

The economic burden on society would have been a tiny fraction of the cleanup and compensation costs had the companies introducing these products acted responsibly. The human casualties would have been avoided, along with the profound community and family disruptions. It was not lack of knowledge, but the lack of corporate interest, that resulted in the transformation of the living environment into the lethal sewers of industry. Interest in controlling the damaging aspects of technology is more likely to come from the potential victims and from parents who care for their children than from the corporate perpetrators. . . .

The environmental movement that questioned . . . chemicals began in earnest as part of the reexamination of values engendered by the war in Vietnam and the civil rights campaign of the early 1960s. Environmentalism offered an alternative to the consumption ethos of the Depression/World War II generation. This alternative was called ecology, after the branch of study that examines the "intricate web of relationships between living organisms and their living and non-living surroundings," as one writer put it. "Ecology" was, at the time, a way of life as much as a science . . .

The need for so many different laws, offering protection from such a broad range of exposures, illustrated how thoroughly dangerous chemicals had dispersed in the environment. The chemical companies had become a large and powerful industry. . . .

This proliferation of chemicals has raised an elemental concern: Is America being poisoned? Questions about the health effects of pollution and chemicals have been raised before. Air pollution combined with atmospheric inversions caused tragedies in several cities, from London, England, to Donora, Pennsylvania, in the late 1940s and early 1950s. In 1958, the Delaney clause (named for New York Congressman James J. Delaney) prohibited the use of food additives proved to cause cancer in "man or animal." . . .

In the mid-1970s the questions raised in the forties, fifties and sixties were answered with chemical disasters that crowded each other off the front page. The synthetic chemicals that appeared after World War II in products of all shapes and sizes also were appearing where they never were meant to be, and often with tragic results. One of those places was the Niagara Falls community of Love Canal. Chemical wastes buried there more than 30 years reached into the lives of hundreds of middle-class families living in neat rows of homes. Women there have had more miscarriages than normal; an unusual number of children have been born with birth defects; serious illnesses have wracked families. Love Canal is the site of the first federal emergency declared in response to a human-made disaster.

Love Canal has brought home the threats of the new industrial era. That synthetic chemicals improperly used or disposed of can cause great harm no longer is a theoretical proposition. The polluted lakes and streams, the fish kills and eyesores of the fifties and sixties were only the first, most visible manifestations; the real impact of the belching smokestacks and autos is being realized only many years later—in the elevated levels of lead measured in the bloodstreams of young children and in the more frequent occurrence of respiratory diseases. The true cost of dirty rivers is revealed in higher rates of cancer among the people who draw their drinking water from those waterways.

At Love Canal, these delayed effects of the new technology have become piercingly evident. And a few months after the public heard about Love Canal, the Three Mile Island nuclear accident sliced through the rhetoric of the nuclear industry. Invulnerability to accident cannot be designed into a reactor. Nor has any means of handling the long-lived nuclear wastes been found; the Three Mile Island accident followed the failure of the nuclear reprocessing plant in West Valley, New York. Evidence mounted of the menace of pesticides. DDT was removed from the market. Other pesticides, too, have been banned. But their residues remain, in the environment and in our bodies. . . .

None of [the] . . . tragedies, however, has turned up in the ledgers of the giant corporations producing the chemicals or of the power plants and steel mills and other industries pouring wastes into the air and water. And this . . . is the essence of the environmental dilemma. Environmental and occupational health regulations have been a belated attempt to assess industries for the true social costs of their products. That accounts for those regulations being so fervently resisted; to want a free ride prolonged forever is natural.

But in the wake of Love Canal and Reserve Mining and Kepone and PCBs and all the other disasters of the decade, the extent of this free ride's cost began to emerge. Protecting the environment was no longer a question only of cleaning up rivers unfit for swimming or of protecting farm lands threatened by suburban sprawl, or even of saving waterfowl endangered by oil spills (though all these remained concerns).

It was a question of saving ourselves.

From Ralph Nader, Ronald Brownstein, and John Richard, eds.,
Who's Poisoning America: Corporate Polluters and Their Victims
in the Chemical Age, **Sierra Club, 1981**

What is it like to work in an industrial plant whose chemicals may poison, cripple, or kill you? Two Southern writers and organizers, Chip Hughes and Len Stanley, went to a plant of the Olin Corporation in North Carolina to find out. Their article first appeared in Southern Exposure, *a journal published by the Institute for Southern Studies, and was later published in a book:*

Next time you open a bag of Fritos or a pack of cigarettes, think about Marvin Gaddy. Marvin has worked in Olin Corporation's Film Division for over twenty years making cellophane wrapping for just about any product you can imagine. He can't see as well as he used to and still gets nightmares every once in a while. He's watched the lives of many men change after they came off his floor. For one man it got so bad he may have taken his own life. Others were luckier and got out with only minor nerve problems to remind them of what it was like up there.

Marvin works in the chemical building at Olin's Film Division near Brevard, North Carolina, on the edge of the Pisgah National Forest. Built in 1951, the Film Division produces viscose which is extruded, solidified, and dried to form cellophane. The second floor houses the xanthation process. Twelve massive barettes are kept in constant rotation, each mixing together seven to eight hundred pounds of ripened alkali cellulose (raw wood pulp and 16 percent caustic acid). Marvin used to add carbon disulfide (CS_2) to the rotating vats, which helped to quicken the process of breaking down the raw wood pulp into a liquid cellophane-like mixture. Nobody ever told Marvin and his fellow workers that the CS_2 could harm them. But they finally found out. Only then it was too late.

"A lot of people would leave," says Marvin.

"The younger ones would come in there, work a few days, and then they'd invariably get a big whiff of CS_2. People would act real unusual, get headaches and think they were getting the flu. After a few overdoses, the nightmares would start coming on them. We'd go in and tell the company, "Dammit, you'd better do something about this CS_2 stuff." They'd tell us to get the hell out—"We don't need you. If you don't enjoy your job, then go home." Course we didn't have a union back then. And we didn't have Jimmy Reese rummaging through their trashcans and filing all those grievances and complaints . . ."

Olin workers had to stand up and fight for more than thirty years before they got the union in. The battle left a trail of beaten-up organizers, fired union sympathizers, and heartbreaking, one-vote Labor Board election defeats. Finally, in 1971, the union won a contract which included a safety committee to monitor working conditions and the in-plant environment. For the past five years, James Reese has used the committee to help his fellow workers investigate numerous toxic substances: asbestos, carbon disulfide, formaldehyde, tetrahydrofuran, flax dust, noise, radiation, methyl bromide. . . .

Congress passed the Williams-Steiger Occupational Safety and Health Act [OSHA] of 1970 in response to escalating on-the-job injury rates and intense pressure from national unions. The act created the OSHA Administration within the U.S. Labor Department, and the responsibility for inspecting the workplace for hazards and imposing penalties of up to $10,000 when unsafe conditions are uncovered. In addition, the act gives bold rights to affected workers to assist them in cleaning up their plants. It is these workers' rights which are the most important aspect of the law, because unions and employees cannot depend on the chronically understaffed and underfinanced OSHA Administration to initiate enforcement. Workers can now file a complaint requesting an unannounced inspection, accompany the OSHA inspector during his inspection, demand an investigation of potentially harmful substances, and even challenge the amount of time given a company to clean up recognized hazards.

For James Reese and the other members of Local 1971, OSHA has become more than another law or bureaucratic agency. It is a tool they can use to take matters into their own hands, a weapon they can hold to the company's head to force them to clean up unhealthy conditions.

Although the hazards of carbon disulfide exposure were recognized as early as 1851 in France, little has been written about the chemical in the United States. Both liquid and vapor are highly irritating to the skin, eyes, nose, and air passages. This local irritation, however, is overshadowed by the serious long-term effects on the body after the chemical has been absorbed through the skin and lungs. High concentrations rapidly affect the brain, causing loss of consciousness, and even death. Lower concentrations may cause headaches and giddiness or lung and stomach irritation.

Prolonged repeated exposures to relatively low levels of CS_2 affect several parts of the body. Brain damage results in mental abnormalities such as depression, euphoria, agitation, hallucinations, and nightmares. Nerve injury can cause blindness when the optic nerve is involved or weakness of the arms and legs when peripheral nerves are inflamed.

From Marc S. Miller, ed., *Working Lives*, Pantheon, 1980

Year by year the public becomes more aware of the world's ecological problems. It was not long ago that most people believed natural resources were infinite. But today, points out John B. Oakes of the New York Times, *"environmental deterioration across the board—from ozone depletion and acid rain to deforestation and extinction of species—is at last becoming recognized as an even greater threat to life on this planet than the nuclear threat it encompasses."*

Taking a look at the American scene, the critic Robert Adams had this to say:

About the landscape of America it's hard to think anymore without a bitter awareness of what it's become.

To spend a night at a grubby cabin at Grand Canyon or Yosemite, one has to make reservations weeks in advance; what one gets to eat is airline food. The high peaks of the Rockies are littered with beer cans and broken glass; the trails are lined with the scars of dead campfires (the wilderness movement having provided its own brand of pollution and contamination). The streams, the lakes, the oceans themselves are awash with garbage. In a serious discussion of transport problems in Connecticut (and not Fairfield County, either), I heard not long ago someone suggesting that all major traffic arteries be double-decked. The idea was absurd, but I wouldn't have been able to suggest a better. People complain of gridlock on the squared-off streets of Manhattan, and they're right; just one day a week (on Sunday, unless there's a parade) the canyon dwellers can come out and see what their city might be like. But in Boston the combination of a haphazard layout, sharply limited space, antiquated public transport, and recent mushroom growth makes the situation even worse than in New York. Everyone in Boston seems to be either lost or stymied or both; new construction plans will apparently disrupt such traffic patterns as there are for the foreseeable future, and in the end dump more thousands of vehicles and people into downtown Boston. . . .

In America at large things are not yet that bad; but it's hard to avoid the conclusion that they are best where there are fewest Americans and least money. It's a sour verdict to render on a once glorious dream, and one would hope the Americanists could help us avoid it. But not by plastering over the ugly facts with verbiage, not by shutting their eyes to hateful reality and musing over a gentler past.

From Robert Adams, *New York Review*, February 16, 1989

As the last decade of the twentieth century was about to begin, a United States Senator, Albert Gore, Jr., summed up the evidence for the imminence of ecological disaster and suggested what the nations of the world might do in a common effort to prevent it:

Humankind has suddenly entered into a brand new relationship with our planet. Unless we quickly and profoundly change the course of our civilization, we face an immediate and grave danger of destroying the worldwide ecological system that sustains life as we know it.

It is time to confront this danger.

In 1939, as clouds of war gathered over Europe, many refused to recognize what was about to happen. No one could imagine a Holocaust, even after shattered glass had filled the streets on Kristallnacht. World leaders waffled and waited, hoping that Hitler was not what he seemed, that world war could be avoided. Later, when aerial photographs revealed death camps, many pretended not to see. Even now, many fail to acknowledge that our victory was not only over Nazism but also over dark forces deep within us.

In 1989, clouds of a different sort signal an environmental holocaust without precedent. Once again, world leaders waffle, hoping the danger will dissipate. Yet today the evidence is as clear as the sounds of glass shattering in Berlin.

Listen:

• The earth's forests are being destroyed at the rate of one football field's worth every second, one Tennessee's worth every year.

• An enormous hole is opening in the ozone layer, reducing the earth's ability to protect life from deadly ultraviolet radiation.

• Living species die at such an unprecedented rate that more than half may disappear within our lifetimes.

• Chemical wastes, in growing volumes, seep downward to poison ground water and upward to destroy the atmosphere's delicate balance.

• Huge quantities of carbon dioxide, methane and chlorofluorocarbons dumped in the atmosphere have trapped heat and raised global temperatures.

• Every day, 37,000 children under the age of 5 die of starvation or preventable diseases made worse by failures of crops and politics.

Why are these dramatic changes taking place? Because the human population is surging; (it took a million years to reach two billion people. In the last 40 years, world population has doubled. And in the next 40 years, the number of people could double again); because the industrial, scientific and technological revolutions magnify the environmental impact of these increases, and because we tolerate self-destructive behavior and environmental vandalism on a global scale. . . .

This crisis is so different from anything before that it is hard to believe it is real. We seize scientific uncertainties, however small, as excuses for inaction. . . . Our complacency stems in part from a standard of living dependent on rapid consumption of the earth's resources. Our generation has inherited the idea that we have the right to appropriate for ourselves the earth's accumulated treasures as quickly as we can consume them. We reach back through millions of years for the deposits that fuel our industrial civilization.

Just as a drug addict needs increasing doses to produce the same effect, our global appetite for the earth's abundance grows each year. We transform the resources of the past into the pollution of the future, telescoping time for self-indulgence in the present.

In 1987, carbon dioxide levels in the atmosphere began to surge with record annual increases. Global temperatures are also climbing: 1987 was the second hottest year on record; 1988 was the hottest. Scientists now predict our current course will raise world temperatures five degrees Celsius in our lifetimes. The last time there was such a shift, it was five degrees colder; New York City was under one kilometer of ice. If five degrees colder over thousands of years produces an ice age, what could five degrees warmer produce in a lifetime?

The 1990's are the decade of decision. Profound changes are required. We must create a new global compact for sustainable development—for example, trading debts for shared environmental stewardship. Our agenda must include the following:

• A worldwide ban in five years on chlorofluorocarbons, which simultaneously destroy the protective ozone layer and cause up to 20 percent of global warming.

• Rapid reductions in carbon dioxide emissions, through increased vehicle mileage standards, increased energy efficiency and development of alternative energy sources.

• A global halt to destruction of forests and swift implementation of worldwide reforestation programs.

• A ban within five years on packaging that is neither recyclable nor naturally degradable, a comprehensive waste minimization program and aggressive efforts to control emissions of methane from landfills and other sources.

• A series of global summit meetings to seek the unprecedented international cooperation the environmental crisis will demand.

In the 1940's, as victory neared over the dark forces unleashed on Kristallnacht, Gen. Omar Bradley offered advice that is once again relevant to the challenge that confronts humanity: "It is time we steered by the stars, not by the lights of each passing ship."

From Albert Gore, Jr., "An Ecological Kristallnacht, Listen,"
New York Times, **March 19, 1989**

The Will to Act

*O*ut of the firsthand experience provided by the documents in this book comes the possibility of many things. It depends in part on what each reader brings to the page. For me, there is the sense of a deep discontent many feel about the way things are. Freedom, equality, justice, fairness—the promise of American life—they are far from being enjoyed by millions. An insatiable desire for growth piles up material goods for the few. Just one percent of Americans now own more than a third of the country's total wealth.

But no amount of wealth, even if it were less unevenly distributed, can meet the nonmaterial needs of the community. The collective movement for ever more things to consume destroys the world of nature and blinds us to any sense of who we really are. And what we might become.

In the voices of some who speak in this book we hear a sadness. A disappointment in how life has turned out. And in some a cynicism that can weaken the resolve to make life better. All around us, every day, is the myth of the free enterprise, down-home, might-makes-right American hero. Life is dramatized as a contest in which the winner takes all. When reality is blurred by such images it is hard to sort out the truth.

It seems reasonable to believe that many of the unfilled needs of Americans would be met if their voices could be heard in the halls of democracy. Many ways have been proposed to accomplish this, but few have been adopted.

Our democracy was established upon a fundamental assumption: The more people who participate, the more creative our society becomes. We must find the means to take hold of our destiny. When working people, farmers, minorities, women, the youth, the aged, the poor—all the people mutuality benefits—come together in the constant struggle to realize the American *promise, government works for them. And they are able to believe that they are the government.*

Can it happen? Look around and you see signs of young people everywhere taking a fresh look at what's going on in their community. In the spring of 1989, 1,200 students came to New York for a four-day conference of the Campus Outreach Opportunity League. It is a national organization for community service and this was its fifth annual conference, attended by a third more students than the previous one. They met to exchange experiences and hear how to get more involved in community betterment. But they did more than talk. They fanned out to some seventy places in the city and on Long Island to tutor poor children, talk to drug addicts, feed the hungry and the homeless, and comfort those dying of AIDS. All of them do work of this kind in their home or college towns. They show a sense of commitment to social causes that reminded their elders of the spirit of the 1960s. Now, however, there is less rhetoric and romanticism and more realism.

Today there is no Vietnam War or civil rights movement to rally young people to action. Sheltered from such struggles and often unaware of that history, young people may become self-absorbed. The others—like those who join a Campus Outreach—do not fool themselves about what they accomplish. They know that giving their help as volunteers to people in trouble does not by itself solve problems. But they learn tough realities, and their desire to do more, a lot more, helps them inspire still others to join in finding ways to make America work for all. Theirs are the ancient virtues: courage, generosity, and the will to act on their beliefs.

CHRONOLOGY

1945   President Roosevelt dies; Vice President Harry Truman
      succeeds him
      United Nations formed
      Atomic bombing of Japan
      World War II ends
      Nuremberg trials

1947   Truman Doctrine and Marshall Plan announced
      Truman launches Loyalty Program
      Justice Department issues "subversives" list
      Families start new movement to suburbs

1948   Truman elected president
      Truman orders desegregation of armed forces

1949   NATO formed
      Communist revolution creates People's Republic of
      China

1950   Move to suburbs changes life patterns for middle and
      working classes
      Economic growth produces abundance of consumer goods
      Large expenditures on research and development turn
      on military applications
      System of alliances and military bases bolsters U.S.
      influence abroad
      Korean War begins
      U.S. begins sending military aid to Vietnam
      Senator McCarthy begins anticommunist campaign
      Internal Security Act passed

1952 Dwight Eisenhower elected president
      McCarran-Walter Act limits visas on political grounds
      H bomb developed

1953 Korean War ends
      Eisenhower issues Security Risk Order

1954 *Brown v. Board of Education* decision by Supreme Court
      bans racial segregation in public schools
      Senate censures McCarthy

1955 Montgomery bus boycott
      Civil rights movement launched
      Alan Ginsberg's *Howl*

1956 Eisenhower reelected president
      Supreme Court upholds ban on segregation in interstate
      bus travel

1957 Soviets put Sputnik in space orbit
      U.S. troops protect black students in desegregation of
      Little Rock high school
      Southern Christian Leadership Conference (SCLC) formed,
      headed by Martin Luther King, Jr.
      Congress passes first Civil Rights Act since 1875

1960 John F. Kennedy elected president
      Student Nonviolent Coordinating Committee (SNCC)
      formed
      Civil Rights Act
      Sit-in movement to desegregate public facilities

1961 U.S. breaks relations with Cuba
      Peace Corps created
      Bay of Pigs invasion

1962   Cuban missile crisis
       John Glenn first American to orbit earth
       Port Huron Statement of Students for a Democratic Soci-
         ety (SDS)
       Rachel Carson's *Silent Spring*
       Michael Harrington's *The Other America*

1963   Assassin kills President Kennedy; Vice President Lyndon
         B. Johnson succeeds him
       Rev. Martin Luther King, Jr., leads March on Washington
         of quarter million blacks and whites for civil rights
       Bob Dylan's "Blowin' in the Wind"
       Betty Friedan's *The Feminine Mystique*
       Nuclear weapons test ban treaty

1964   President Johnson elected to continue in office
       Civil Rights Act of 1964 outlaws racial discrimination in
         all public accommodations
       Tonkin Gulf Resolution gives president power to send
         more troops to Vietnam
       Mississippi Freedom Summer Project
       Three civil rights workers murdered in Mississippi
       Free Speech Movement at Berkeley
       Beatles begin tours of America

1965   President Johnson's Great Society programs—Medicare,
         Medicaid, water quality, higher education, housing and
         immigration acts—adopted by Congress
       Voting Rights Act wipes out all restrictions on voting
       U.S. sends first combat troops to Vietnam
       Campus teach-ins on Vietnam War
       Selma-to-Montgomery march dramatizes black voting
         rights
       Malcolm X shot to death

1966   National Organization for Women (NOW) founded
       "Black Power" slogan becomes national issue
       Riots in several urban ghettos
       Cesar Chavez–led grape-picker strike in California

1967   Six-Day War between Israel and Arab nations ends with
       Israel occupying large new territories
       Demonstration against Vietnam War on Pentagon steps
       Thurgood Marshall first black Supreme Court Justice

1968   Richard M. Nixon elected president
       Campus upheavals begin at Columbia
       Martin Luther King, Jr., assassinated; riots in 125 cities
       My Lai massacre in Vietnam
       Robert Kennedy assassinated
       National Environmental Policy Act

1969   U.S. astronauts land on moon
       Movement for homosexual rights emerges
       Woodstock Festival

1970s Technological developments: Explorer I launched in or-
       bit; computers marketed commercially; Viking probe
       of moon; genetic engineering; lasers; artificial joints
       and organs advance medicine

1970   Americans begin moving to Sunbelt
       U.S. bombs Cambodia
       Congress repeals Tonkin Gulf Resolution
       Students killed during protests at Kent State and Jackson
       State universities
       Earth Day launches environmental mass movement

1971   Pentagon Papers published
       Supreme Court rules unanimously that busing of students
          may be ordered to achieve racial desegregation
       Twenty-sixth Amendment to U.S. Constitution lowers
          voting age to eighteen

1972   Nixon visits China and Soviet Union
       Equal Rights Amendment (ERA) passes Congress
       U.S. and USSR sign arms limitation treaty
       Burglars caught breaking into Democratic headquarters
          in Watergate complex, Washington, D.C.; Watergate
          investigation begins

1973   Cease-fire agreement in Vietnam
       October War in Middle East
       Arab oil embargo

1974   Nixon resigns under threat of impeachment, first presi-
          dent to do so; Gerald Ford becomes president

1975   Vietnam War ends
       Helsinki accords on human rights signed

1976   Bicentennial celebration of Independence
       Jimmy Carter elected president

1977   United States and USSR among fifteen nations signing
          pact curbing spread of nuclear weapons

1979   Three Mile Island nuclear accident
       U.S. recognizes China
       Soviet troops invade Afghanistan

Camp David accords between Israel and Egypt
SALT II agreement signed by U.S. and USSR
Iranians seize American hostages

1980 Ronald Reagan elected president
      More women begin to work outside the home

1981 Sandra Day O'Connor first woman named to Supreme
      Court
      Reagan introduces supply-side economics
      American hostages released by Iran
      Reports of AIDS confirmed

1982 ERA fails ratification

1985 Arms control talks resume
      Mikhail Gorbachev, new leader of USSR, begins summit
      meetings with Reagan

1986 Scientists report finding AIDS virus
      Major nuclear accident at USSR's Chernobyl power
      station
      Secret Iran-Contra operations revealed
      Illegal insider trading on Wall Street exposed

1987 Thousands of aliens seek legal status under new amnesty
      law
      Wall Street suffers worst stock market drop in history
      U.S. trade deficit sets record
      Two hundred thousand supporters of gay and lesbian
      rights demonstrate in capital for more federal money to
      combat AIDS and for an end to discrimination

Congressional committee report charges Reagan failed to obey constitutional requirement to execute laws and bears "ultimate responsibility" for wrongdoing by aides in sale of arms to Iran and diversion of funds to Nicaraguan rebels

Reagan and Gorbachev sign arms control treaty

1988 U.S. and USSR sign accord on joint scientific research
George Bush elected president

1989 Hurrican Hugo causes great damage in Puerto Rico and Southeastern States

Earthquake rocks San Fransico-Oakland, California, region

USSR, under the leadership of Mikhail Gorbachev, begins to move away from one-party dictatorship and relaxes its grip on East European Satelite nations; nonvoilent revolutions in these nations end Communist Party rule and open the way for democracy and free-market economies

ACKNOWLEDGMENTS

Acknowledgment is gratefully made for permission to quote from the following works: Speech by Dr. Howard Hiatt, from *Confrontations*, Winter, 1981, reprinted by permission of Dr. Howard Hiatt. Excerpt from *Peekskill, USA, A Personal Experience*, by Howard Fast, copyright © 1951 by Howard Fast, reprinted by permission of Howard Fast. Excerpt from *The Military Half*, by Jonathan Schell, Alfred A. Knopf, Inc., copyright © 1968, reprinted by permission of Alfred A. Knopf, Inc. Excerpt from *Prison Journals of a Priest Revolutionary*, by Philip Berrigan, compiled and edited by Vincent McGee, copyright © 1967, 1968, 1969, 1970 by Philip Berrigan, reprinted by permission of Henry Holt & Co., Inc. Excerpts on Jean Gump, Mary Gonzales, Chris Nearmyer and Douglas Roth from *The Great Divide*, by Studs Terkel, Pantheon, copyright © 1988, by permission of Random House. Excerpts on Ruby Hurley, Franklin McCain and Hank Thomas from *My Soul Is Rested: Movement Days in the Deep South Remembered by Howell Raines*, copyright © 1977 by Howell Raines, reprinted by permission of the Putnam Publishing Group. Excerpts from "Police Embody Racism to My People," by Don Jackson, *New York Times*, January 23, 1989, and "Unlikely AIDS Sufferer's Message: Even You Can Get It," by Bruce Lambert, *New York Times*, March 11, 1989, copyright © 1989 by The New York Times Company, reprinted by permission. Excerpts on Jodean Culbert, Vine Deloria, Joe Begley, and Jenny de la Cruz from *American Dreams*, by Studs Terkel, Pantheon, copyright © 1980, by permission of Random House. Excerpts from *American Journey*, by Richard Reeves, copyright © 1982 by Richard Reeves, by permission of Simon & Schuster, Inc. Excerpt from *The Feminine Mystique*, by Betty Friedan, copyright © 1963 by Betty

Friedan, reprinted by permission of W. W. Norton & Co. Inc. Excerpt by Ronnie Lichtman, from *Up from Under*, May–June 1970, reprinted by permission of Ronnie Lichtman. Excerpt from *The Other America*, by Michael Harrington, copyright © 1962 by Michael Harrington, reprinted with permission of Macmillan Publishing Co. Excerpt from article of Alex Kotlowitz, *The Wall Street Journal*, October 27, 1987, reprinted by permission of *The Wall Street Journal*. Excerpt from *Silent Spring*, by Rachel Carson, copyright © 1962 by Rachel Carson, reprinted with permission of Houghton Mifflin. Excerpt from *Who's Poisoning America*, by Ralph Nader, copyright © 1981 by Ralph Nader, reprinted by permission of Sierra Club Books. Excerpt from essay by R. M. Adams, *The New York Review of Books*, February 16, 1989, copyright © 1989 by Nyrev, Inc., reprinted with permission by *The New York Review of Books*. Excerpt from "An Ecological Kristallnacht, Listen," by Albert Gore, Jr., *The New York Times*, March 19, 1989, copyright © 1989 by The New York Times Company, reprinted by permission.

INDEX